GLOBAL ISSUES BIBLE STUDIES

Series editors: Stephen Hayner & Gordon Aeschliman

LEADERSHIP IN THE 21ST CENTURY

Gordon Aeschliman

6 Studies
for individuals
or groups

D0067788

INTERVARSITY PRESS
DOWNERS GROVE, ILLINOIS 60515

InterVarsity Press is the book-publishing division of InterVarsity Christian Fellowship, a student movement active on campus at hundreds of universities, colleges and schools of nursing in the United States of America, and a member movement of the International Fellowship of Evangelical Students. For information about local and regional activities, write Public Relations Dept., InterVarsity Christian Fellowship, 6400 Schroeder Rd., P.O. Box 7895, Madison, WI 53707-7895.

All Scripture quotations, unless otherwise indicated, are from the Holy Bible, New International Version. Copyright © 1973, 1978, International Bible Society. Used by permission of Zondervan Bible Publishers.

Cover illustration: TransLight

ISBN 0-8308-4902-5

Printed in the United States of America

12	11	10	9	8	7	6	5	4	3	2	1
99	98	97	96	95	94	93	92	91	90		

Contents

Because humankind is made in the image of God, every person, regardless of race, religion, color, culture, class, sex or age, has an intrinsic dignity because of which he or she should be respected and served, not exploited. Here too we express penitence both for our neglect and for having sometimes regarded evangelism and social concern as mutually exclusive.

Although reconciliation with people is not reconciliation with God, nor is social action evangelism, nor is political liberation salvation, nevertheless we affirm that evangelism and sociopolitical involvement are both part of our Christian duty. For both are necessary expressions of our doctrines of God and humankind, our love for our neighbor and our obedience to Jesus Christ.

The message of salvation implies also a message of judgment upon every form of alienation, oppression and discrimination, and we should not be afraid to denounce evil and injustice wherever they exist.

—Lausanne Covenant, Article Five.

Welcome to Global Issues Bible Studies

With all the rapid and dramatic changes happening in our world today, it's easy to be overwhelmed and simply withdraw. But it need not be so for Christians! God has not only given us the mandate to love the world, he has given us the Holy Spirit and the community of fellowship to guide us and equip us in the ministry of love.

Ministering in the world can be threatening: It requires change in both our lifestyle and our thinking. We end up discovering that we need to cling closer to Jesus than ever before—and that becomes the great personal benefit of change. God's love for the world is the same deep love he has for you and me.

This study series is designed to help us understand what is going on in *the world*. Then it takes us to *the Word* to help us be faithful in our compassionate response. The series is firmly rooted in the evangelical tradition which calls for a personal saving relationship with Jesus Christ and a public lifestyle of discipleship that demonstrates the Word has truly come alive in us.

At the front of the guide is an excerpt from the Lausanne Covenant which we have found particularly helpful. We have developed this series in keeping with the spirit of the covenant, especially sections four and five. You may wish to refer to the Lausanne Covenant for further guidance as you form your own theology of evangelism and social concern.

In the words of the covenant's authors we place this challenge before you: "The salvation we claim should be transforming us in the totality of our personal and social responsibilities. Faith without works is dead."

Getting the Most from Global Issues Bible Studies
Global Issues Bible Studies are designed to be an exciting and challenging way to help us seek God's will for all of the world as it is found in Scripture. As we learn more about the world, we will learn more about ourselves as well.

How They Are Designed
Global Issues Bible Studies have a number of distinctive features. First, each guide has an introduction from the author which will help orient us to the subject at hand and the significant questions which the studies will deal with.

Second, the Bible study portion is inductive rather than deductive. In other words, the author will lead us to discover what the Bible says about a particular topic through a series of questions rather than simply telling us what he or she believes. Therefore, the studies are thought-provoking. They help us to think about the meaning of the passage so that we can truly understand what the biblical writer intended to say.

Third, the studies are personal. Global Issues Bible Studies are not just theoretical studies to be considered in private or discussed in a group. These studies will motivate us to action. They will expose us to the promises, assurances, exhortations and challenges of God's

Word. Through the study of Scripture, we will renew our minds so that we can be transformed by the Spirit of God.

Fourth, the guides include resource sections that will help you to act on the challenges Scripture has presented you with.

Fifth, these studies are versatile. They are designed for student, mission, neighborhood and/or church groups. They are also effective for individual study.

How They Are Put Together

Global Issues Bible Studies also have a distinctive format. Each study need take no more than forty-five minutes in a group setting or thirty minutes in personal study—unless you choose to take more time.

Each guide has six studies. If the guides are used in pairs, they can be used within a quarter system in a church and fit well in a semester or trimester system on a college campus.

The guides have a workbook format with space for writing responses to each question. This is ideal for personal study and allows group members to prepare in advance for the discussion. In addition the last question in each study offers suggestions and opportunity for personal response.

At the end of the guides are some notes for leaders. They describe how to lead a group discussion, give helpful tips on group dynamics and suggest ways to deal with problems which may arise during the discussion. With such helps, someone with little or no experience can lead an effective study.

Suggestions for Individual Study

1. As you begin the study, pray that God will help you understand and apply the passages to your life. Pray that he will show you what kinds of action he would have you take as a result of your time of study.

2. In your first session take time to read the introduction to the entire guide. This will orient you to the subject at hand and the author's goals for the studies.

3. Read the short introduction to the study.

4. Read and reread the suggested Bible passages to familiarize yourself with them.

5. A good modern translation of the Bible, rather than the King James Version or a paraphrase, will give you the most help. The New International Version, the New American Standard Bible and the Revised Standard Version are all recommended. The questions in this guide are based on the New International Version.

6. Use the space provided to respond to the questions. This will help you express your understanding of the passage clearly.

7. Look up the passages listed under *For Further Study* at the end of each study. This will help you to better understand the principles outlined in the main passages and give you an idea of how these themes are found throughout Scripture.

8. It might be good to have a Bible dictionary handy. Use it to look up any unfamiliar words, names or places.

9. Take time with the final question in each study to commit yourself to action and/or a change in attitude.

Suggestions for Group Study

1. Come to the study prepared. Follow the suggestions for individual study mentioned above. You will find that careful preparation will greatly enrich your time spent in group discussion.

2. Be willing to participate in the discussion. The leader of your group will not be lecturing. Instead, he or she will be encouraging the members of the group to discuss what they have learned. The leader will be asking the questions that are found in this guide.

3. Stick to the topic being discussed. Your answers should be based on the verses which are the focus of the discussion and not on outside authorities such as commentaries or speakers.

4. Be sensitive to the other members of the group. Listen attentively when they describe what they have learned. You may be surprised by their insights! When possible, link what you say to the comments of others. Also, be affirming whenever you can. This will encourage

some of the more hesitant members of the group to participate.

5. Be careful not to dominate the discussion. We are sometimes so eager to express our thoughts that we leave too little opportunity for others to respond. By all means participate! But allow others to also.

6. Expect God to teach you through the passage being discussed and through the other members of the group. Pray that you will have an enjoyable and profitable time together, but also that as a result of the study, you will find ways that you can take action individually and/or as a group.

7. If you are the discussion leader, you will find additional suggestions at the back of the guide.

God bless you in your adventure of love.

Steve Hayner
Gordon Aeschliman

Introducing Leadership in the 21st Century

I was born and raised in the Republic of South Africa.

White government and White church leaders there pleaded passionately with us to assist them in their agenda to "protect the nation from Black communist-inspired terrorists." Newspapers and magazines were banned from publishing the conditions of Black life under White rule, and it was considered treason to speak with certain Black leaders. Christian leaders would arrogantly and vehemently defend the White system. Yet almost none of them had ever been inside a Black township. All of their debate and "moral" platforming was based on the fables of leaders who clung selfishly to White rule and power. These leaders were nothing more than the uninformed pawns of the politicians.

Most missionaries didn't do much better. They believed, all too often, the government propaganda which said that communism was behind Black freedom aspirations. Black Christian leaders who pressed for justice and equality were labeled by White missionaries as "uppity" and "liberal." Who were they to inform these visiting evangelists of the moral demands of the gospel in Black squalor? Yes, missionaries at least went to Black neighborhoods, but mostly to preach and counsel, rarely to be taught.

This scenario is repeated countless times around the world today. Third World Christian leaders are exasperated by the haughtiness and deaf ears of White Christian leaders who come to their countries stuffed full of words to give, with no room left to learn.

In the face of situations as complex as that of South Africa, what is the Christian leader called to do? And as our world becomes more and more complicated in the century to come, who will the leaders be?

What Is Leadership?

Leadership should not be modeled after the few "mega-ministries" in North America. These multimillion-dollar organizations are heavily invested in their donors. The organizations do not seem to be looking for leaders to come in and chart new territory and introduce change in concert with the changing world. Most are looking for managers— people gifted with the skills to keep the machinery running and maintain a healthy relationship with contributors. This is not leadership.

Instead, leadership is much more subtle and certainly much more profound than we have realized. Its expressions are as diverse as the personalities God has created, and the opportunities for its exertion are endless.

The predominant secular definition of a leader is one "who is able to corral and steer large numbers of people in one direction." The larger the number, the greater the leader. Christian leadership has nothing to borrow from that definition. The Christian leader is, quite simply, the person who, by example, is able to lead others to live lives that reflect kingdom values. Sounds too simple, doesn't it? Unfortunately, we have been misled to believe that the chief word in the phrase "Christian leader" is *leader,* whereas it is actually *Christian.* The consequences of this error are not pretty: "Christian" televangelists are known to have swindled millions from their donors. "Christian" preachers support racist laws that oppress millions of Black South Africans. "Christian" mission leaders slander other mission leaders, while calling for more missionaries. The world of the fast-approaching twenty-first century is desperately in need of Christian leaders who are first "Christian."

We need to restore dignity to the role of the biblical leader—not the person whose leadership is measured statistically. The biblical leader is the mother or father who raises a godly family, the campus leader who demands just treatment of minorities, or the layperson who presses the elders to organize care for the local homeless. This leader is the daughter or son who leaves family to communicate the Good News crossculturally, the CEO who declines certain economic opportunities that exploit women, and the pastor who stays in the ghetto because of his or her conviction that God has a special concern for the poor and less privileged.

Put in simple terms, the single most important dimension of leadership (and perhaps most overlooked) is the moral courage to live an ethical life. This call to leadership is open to all Christians. Similarly, leadership in the Christian sense is forfeited at the point where one's public influence outpaces one's private ethical living.

Given this backdrop, it's important now to understand what particular demands are placed on the leader who is about to enter the world of the twenty-first century.

An Inquiring Mind

As demonstrated by the example of South Africa, Christian leaders have the moral duty to know what's going on in the world. In Matthew 25 we have the picture of people who claim innocence before God because they hadn't "seen" the hungry, the prisoner or the orphan. God isn't very understanding—he banishes them to outer darkness.

We cannot operate from the assumption that we have no more to learn. Instead, we must be hungry to know. We have no right to hold or defend uninformed opinions. A Bible-school diploma does not qualify us to fly into the complexities of another nation's history, politics, culture and religious practices with our prepackaged sermons and strategies.

We haven't even been able to hear the cries of "racism" and "foul play" from our own ethnic Christian leaders in the United States. We label their agendas "irrelevant" and "tangential" to our Christian mission—how in the world do we expect to hear the words of leaders on the other side of the globe?

The Christian leaders of the twenty-first century should be marked by their humble, teachable spirits. They will need an almost uncanny ability to avoid being swayed by their own national or political affiliations, a high regard for others' opinions and histories, and an insatiable desire to understand the world as it really is.

A few of these leaders will assume responsibility for the direction of the mega-ministries. But by far the majority will be the undocumented millions of men and women who repeatedly point us back in the direction of the kingdom of God and whose very lives interpret for us what it means to be a child of God in today's crooked and broken world.

Living in the Tension

The word *balance* has taken on the implied meanings "normal," "average" and "between the extremes." None of these describes the Christian lifestyle.

We are, according to the Bible, at war—with our flesh, the old self, the world's systems, the heavenlies—and the temptation to step out of that fight is always with us. Therefore, most of us tend toward the path of least resistance. We settle into a routine of Christian living that eventually does not look much different from the daily routine of making the bed and driving to work.

Christian leaders face this temptation as much as anyone.

Living in the tension between the Spirit and the world requires a few commitments. The first is living with a dynamic interaction between the world and the Word. This posture assumes that we don't know it all, that the Word of God is an unfathomable treasure chest that literally changes us from glory to glory the more we plumb its depths. This posture also assumes that Scripture is alive and active in the world and that our understanding of God's Word is given clarity and new insight as we live out our Christianity in the midst of the despairing, grimy, complex and ever-changing world.

Essentially, we are called to enter into an argument, an ongoing dialog between the world and the Word. We are "anchored to the Rock," as Youth for Christ's motto says, not anchored to the level of understanding we had ten years ago. The leaders of the twenty-first century must be people whose careful reading of the Word drives them out, almost involuntarily, into the middle of the world's pain. There they can minister the mercy, grace and justice of the God they have come to know in the Word. But then the pain of the world breaks their hearts anew, and they throw themselves afresh into God's Word, anxious to find answers to questions that they had not asked before. They receive new insights, and once again they are thrust into the world's pain.

And so the cycle continues, like a never-ending spiral: deeper in the Word, deeper into the world's pain.

Our understanding of God's call on the church to engage the world with his love is not a static enterprise. Rather, it's a dynamic, changing enterprise that should regularly leave us a little more humbled and awed at how high, how long, how deep and how wide is the love of God.

We must be clear that this dynamic interaction between the Word and the world is not simply a question of strategy—although it is partially that. Surely the more we step inside another's world, the more we will realize the need to adjust our forms of ministry in order to be more effective. That is good strategy. But this dynamic interaction also calls for us to grow in our understanding of the substance of our mission to the world. It's arrogant for any of us to assume that we have arrived at the pure, unadulterated understanding of God's love.

If we are to live in the tension, we will also need to commit ourselves to letting go and living with ambiguity. There is something very secure in holding onto a world that is envisioned in black-and-white terms—Republican versus Democrat, socialist versus capitalist, Free World versus Marxist, liberal versus conservative, terrorist versus freedom fighter. Eventually, we become servants to the banner we fly over our tents. But Christ's should be the only name that elicits our allegiance.

In reality, the world does not fall into tidy categories. If we choose to grow, we will regularly discover that some of our assumptions about the Christian mission are more cultural and hand-me-down doctrines than actual biblical mandates. Letting go is threatening because our goals and relationships will be affected if we're willing to change. The natural tendency is to grasp that which has become familiar. But then we are not simply "natural" people. We need to be leaders who have the moral courage to adjust our world views and structures in step with our ethical development. This is true integrity.

Leaders who have the capability of accepting the ambiguity of living in the tension while "anchored to the Rock" will be the leaders who guard the Western church from becoming an irrelevant vestige of once-noble dreams and visions that have outlived their purposes.

Biblically Literate

"Your word is a lamp to my feet and a light for my path." David knew the value of God's recorded Word. Several of his psalms are nothing more than a celebration of his love for the Word—he considered it honey, a banquet table, a priceless treasure.

One great distinguishing mark of the leader of the twenty-first century must be a love affair with the Scriptures, a love that leads to an astute awareness of its completeness and worthiness in guiding us into all truth and into godly lives. The Bible needs to be the most dog-eared, pored-over, prayed-through, cried-upon book in our possession.

The world has shrunk to the size of a city, given the advances of technology and transportation. Every conceivable religious and secular system is being broadcast from the town square. If we do not understand how all of Scripture hangs together in a unified view of Creator and creation, our ability to communicate to all of the world will be jeopardized. We cannot expect to answer the legitimate questions posed by other systems of this world if we have not pursued the Word.

Christian activists—those calling for our commitment to forcefully living out the biblical mandate in society—must get beyond single-track theologizing. We must discover how church planting and seeking justice for the oppressed are both part of God's call to us. God willing, the twenty-first century will witness a mainstream of leaders who love the Bible more than traditions and, consequently, embrace a theology in which life and mission work together.

There are no pop-up answers. Being biblically literate includes a working knowledge of Scripture that can be applied to all of life—not just prooftexting to help us prove our point.

The Bible's pages give words to our wonderment as we contemplate the majesty of a mountain range and the beauty of snow silently laying its blanket over pine trees. There we discover the tender heart of God for those created in his image, and the anger of a just and terrible Father who hates those who oppress his sons and daughters. We experience the brokenness of those confronted by their sin and the joy of those set free from it.

Becoming biblically literate is an exciting journey that does not have to end until the Author takes us home. And being familiar with Scripture will equip us to leave the Author's fingerprints wherever we reach out to touch the estranged and crippled world.

Community

Finally, the new leaders of the twenty-first century must be men and women who are not dazzled by the appeal of the celebrity-out-front. Instead, leadership must be in part a celebration of how diverse the family is and a demonstration of how dependent we are on those diverse giftings.

The heart of the gospel takes on form as we come together to explore life in Christ. Poor and rich, White and Black, women and men, South and North—these are gifts to us, dimensions of the image of God that belong to our identity as Christians and our understanding of his Word. We all bring our unique histories and experiences that have shed light on portions of the Scriptures that others-in-Christ would not be able to see without us. God is both learned and expressed in this multicultural getting together.

The world of the twenty-first century is only days away from us. It is both an exciting and a despairing field that waits for people willing to step courageously into unknown territories. We must ask ourselves: Are we willing to be untethered from our secure moorings, our cultural and theological "golden cows," that keep us from the challenge of the world before us?

In the Old Testament we find that Esther was ready to respond to God's call. May our lives agree with her awe-filled proclamation of some 2,500 years ago: "To think that I have been brought into the kingdom through God's grace for such a time as this!"

Study 1

An Affair of the Heart

Too often we confuse doing things for God with drawing close to God. Some of us have been misled to think of God as a sort of cosmic taskmaster who measures our worth by our deeds. If our identities become wrapped up in noble plans to reach the world, ultimately— and ironically—our self-created tasks become our masters.

God has called us instead to a deep and passionate love relationship with him. Our identity is as his beloved, and all other loves and good works flow from that Love.

The call that recurs most often in Scripture is for us to love God with all our heart, soul, mind and strength. It should not surprise us, then, that God employs rather harsh language against Israel for betraying his love.

Read Ezekiel 11:16-21.

1. God tells the Israelites that they must remove the "vile images" and "detestable idols" from the land before he works on their hearts (vv. 18-19). Why do you suppose he puts that requirement on them up front?

2. What would modern-day idols and images look like?

3. What is an "undivided heart" (v. 19)?

4. Ezekiel tells us that the Lord has said of idol worshippers, "I will bring down on their own heads what they have done" (v. 21). What does this mean?

Read Ezekiel 16:1-34 for a picture of God's response to betrayed love.
5. Contrast the "undivided heart" of Ezekiel 11:19 with the picture

described in Ezekiel 16:15-29.

6. List the three outcomes of an undivided heart.

7. A "heart of flesh" is an image of compassion, a tenderness that can feel the pain of the world, in contrast to a heart of stone that has no feelings. Give one example of how our loving God has softened your heart.

8. Following the decrees of God is also a consequence of an undivided heart. Describe how our loving God has led to obedience in your life.

9. Community, a sense of belonging, also results from a heart refined by God's love. Compare Ezekiel 11:20 to Titus 2:14 and describe

God's desire for relationship.

What is the prerequisite for a deep relationship with God?

Read 1 John 2:15-17.
10. Ezekiel 11:19-21 is repeated, in a fashion, in 1 John 2:15-17. Describe three ways in which devotion to God will lead us to say no to the world.

11. *Leadership question:* What forms of infidelity are currently blocking your love relationship with God?

12. *Response:* Identify the influences or forces in your life that tend to make obedience and works, rather than love, the basis of your relationship with God.

For Further Study: Hosea 2; Jeremiah 2; Luke 16:13 and Ephesians 3:14-21.

Study 2

Concrete Love

Love can be a fuzzy concept.

For some it is a wild inner force that drives them to conquer foreign kingdoms to win the affections of a princess. For others, it's an equally wild engine fueled by hormones whose only destiny appears to be the bedroom.

Love may be a poem or a sunset. Or it may be a daily routine of making beds and washing clothes, of combing a child's hair and putting bread on the table. Or perhaps love is playing footsie under the candlelit table and making promises in an atmosphere of mellow jazz bands and champagne bubbles.

Human emotions are a gift from God. They bring tenderness to our world, interpret our experiences, help us unlock heart chambers that conceal our deepest hurts and hold our most powerful thoughts. And they give us energy to pursue our noblest dreams and visions.

But love is much more than all of these. Love is the very nature of God—that unfathomable tenderness that drove Jesus to the cross and that continues to drive him to pursue us.

Love is absolutely central to our identity as Christians. The Scriptures tell us that all the requirements of the Law and the Prophets are summed up in the two great commands to love God and our neighbor.

Love is not a fuzzy concept in reality. It is demanding. It requires concrete response: "If you love me, you will keep my commandments." "If you love me, you will lay down your life."

When we give our lives to Christ, we enter into a lifestyle of love. At that point, the needs of the world place a moral demand on us to live in a way that reflects the love of Christ. And that response is concrete.

Read 1 John 3—4.

1. Scripture says that the evidence that supports our having passed from death to life is that we love our brothers and sisters (3:14). What evidence in your own life suggests that you have moved from death to life?

2. We cannot claim to love God whom we have not seen, and yet hate our brother or sister whom we have seen (4:20). Loving God appears to be inseparable from loving others. Explain the implications of not loving your brother or sister.

3. "All that matters is your attitude." This statement is commonly made regarding the accumulation of wealth and possessions in the face of poverty and world need. In light of this passage what do you think of this perspective?

4. What distinction is the apostle John making in 3:18?

Provide specific examples of how this distinction works.

5. Love demands concrete response from us. What demand does 1 John 3:17 place on you? Be specific.

6. God so loved the world that he gave his only Son to die for us (4:10). Jesus is our supreme example of how to love. He said to us, "As the Father sent me, so send I you." How has your life so far reflected "being sent"?

Read Luke 10:25-37.

7. The Good Samaritan story depicts three people who knew of the specific need of another. How did each person respond?

What did Jesus have to say about it (v. 37)?

8. Westerners have no shortage of information regarding the needs of today's world. What might it mean to be modern-day priests or Levites who are "in the know" but do nothing?

9. *Leadership question:* Identify two cultural forces that work against your commitment to concrete love. What have you learned in this study that can help you confront those cultural forces as you seek to be faithful in loving others as God has loved you?

10. *Response:* What specific needs in the world today demand concrete, loving response from you?

How are you going to respond to them?

For Further Study: Matthew 25:31-46 and James 5:1-6.

Study 3

Wholesome Care

Some *Christian leaders have put forward a view that ultimately we* are called only to evangelism and church-planting. However, such a perspective propagates a truncated gospel that causes us to ignore the cries and pain of the world's people—because ultimately the returning King will take care of those needs.

Christ's love is all-encompassing. A very quick reading of Scripture shows how his compassion is readily stirred for the hungry, the homeless and the orphans, and how hot his temper rages against those who oppress.

God's love is restless to care for all the pain and brokenheartedness in society, and we are called to be instruments of that love. He is constantly redeeming all of us and all the world. He's the perfect parent whose wholesome love knows no boundary of mercy and justice.

The cries of the twenty-first century must be heard by Christians who understand that deep love.

Read Isaiah 58.
1. How was Israel expressing its spirituality (v. 3)?

2. Nowhere does God actually say that those forms are wrong; none-theless, he is angry at Israel. Why? (Notice both what they did do and what they did not do—vv. 3-7.)

3. How will God respond to correct fasting (vv. 8-14)?

Read Luke 4:14-21.
4. This passage is Jesus' introduction of his ministry. According to verses 18-19, what is Jesus' mission?

5. It should not be surprising that Jesus' introduction of himself reflects a very broad concern. How does this announcement compare

to God's requirements for true fasting in Isaiah 58?

6. Picture in your mind what Jesus' ministry would look like in our culture. Describe what that ministry would be like.

7. *Leadership question:* What commitments can you make to live differently as concrete evidence that God cares for the whole person?

8. *Response:* How does your ministry encompass all of the elements which Jesus includes in Luke 4:18-19?

For Further Study: Matthew 9:35-38.

Study 4

Christian Character

We live in an age where "Christian leaders" can quite simply be created with the help of wealth and technology. Men and women, in the name of Christ, are wielding great influence over the lives of hundreds of thousands of believers.

And yet their own lives may be in moral shambles.

A true Christian leader is one whose public moral influence is simply an extension of a deeply nurtured and mature innermost private life in Christ.

The rapid pace of modern society often forces us to react on the spot out of who we already are. To meet these demands we must rely on the much deeper resource of the Spirit. How we are guided becomes a reflection of our core values.

We need a fresh call to the holiness and integrity of the Christian way.

Reread 1 John 3.

1. "No one who is born of God will continue to sin" (3:9). Describe, providing evidence, how you have been born of God.

2. "Anyone who does not do what is right is not a child of God" (3:10). God simply declares that we do not belong to him if sin marks our lives. The apostle John is speaking in very clear "black-and-white" terms here. What is the heart of his message in this passage?

3. List the images in chapter 3 that describe new life (vv. 6, 9, 14-15, 24).

4. How do these images relate to your understanding of what it means to be born again?

5. The development of our Christian character is inseparable from our identity as people born from a pure seed. In what ways does chapter 3 suggest that our character development requires action on our part (vv. 4, 10, 18, 22-24)?

Read 1 Peter 1:13—2:3.
6. What similarities do you see between the message of this passage and that of 1 John 3?

7. What elements in 1:13 are important to Christian leadership?

8. List five specific outcomes of a life born of imperishable seed (2:1).

Read 1 John 1:5-7.
9. What, in your opinion, does it mean to "walk in the darkness" (v. 6)?

10. "There is no darkness in God." That statement puts all sin on an equal footing—that is, it is all unacceptable for those born of God. What sins do you think Christians tend to judge as worse than others (for example, sexual sin versus slander)?

11. How does our Christian witness relate to our Christian character?

12. *Leadership question:* The development of our Christian character is ultimately the outcome of falling deeply in love with Jesus. Jesus calls himself the "light of the world" (Jn 8:12), and we are called to love the light (Jn 3:19-21). David said of God, "The LORD turns my darkness into light" (2 Sam 22:29). Describe how your life in Christ can actually become a light to the world.

13. *Response:* Many of us have been disappointed by leaders in high places who fell morally. What accountability structures could you implement to help you keep pursuing the development of a godly character? Act on it.

Study 5

Servant Calling

Leaders *of Christian ministries face the danger of promoting their* particular cause at the expense of love and servanthood.

Too often our ministries could be described as sick bodies, racked by the fever of malicious talk, conceit, disunity, jealousy, striving, and empire-building. The holiness and peace of God have often been sacrificed to the extension of our organizations.

Jesus flatly denies that those practices originate in his kingdom—they are deeds of darkness rather than light. The sobering picture of wood, hay and stubble being consumed in the final day applies to the results of our leadership.

We must pray that the leaders of the twenty-first century will have a jealousy for a deep bond of love and unity, and that our desire to be God's servants to the body and the world will always outstrip our sense of self-importance.

Read Philippians 1:1-6.
1. To whom is the letter addressed (v. 1)?

2. What word does Paul use to describe his relationship with the Philippian Christians (v. 4)?

3. What understanding can you gain from this passage about the distinction between full-time Christian workers and laypersons (vv. 2, 5)?

Read Philippians 2.
4. Service to the world begins with experiencing God's love for us. How does Paul describe that love (vv. 2-5)?

5. How does Paul make the connection between being loved by God and loving others?

6. What does he caution against in verses 3-4? Give specific examples of what these behaviors look like.

7. How does Paul contrast these behaviors with Jesus' example (vv. 5-8)?

8. Paul refers to himself as a "drink offering" in verse 17. What do you suppose he means by that?

9. What are Timothy's strengths (vv. 19-22)? Compare them with the description of Jesus in verses 6-9.

10. How is Epaphroditus described in verses 25-30?

11. *Leadership question:* Just as there is no darkness in Christ, there is no ministry in Christ's name aside from humble, loving servanthood. How do you want your life to change to reflect this truth?

12. *Response:* The Scriptures say that we can even give our bodies to be burned at the stake, but without love we are nothing (1 Cor 13). The outward signs of servanthood are not really the issue with God. The issue is the substance of who I have become—that is, a true servant. What inside your heart is preventing you from being more of a servant?

What worldly values work against servanthood in your life? Ask God to intervene.

Study 6

Courage

Courage is the resolve to be God's moral person in the midst of a world and a church so entangled in compromise that they don't recognize right from wrong.

We need to be a people who can say with the writer of Hebrews, "But we are not of those who shrink back and are destroyed, but of those who believe and are saved."

One of the costliest and loneliest dimensions of leadership is the courage to go as God has called—against the seductive cowardice of a society that has elected to go its own way.

The prophets of the Old Testament were called primarily to the nation of Israel—that body of people blessed with the revelation and special attention of God. Yet these people constantly shrank back from the call to go God's way, and eventually they lost God's blessings.

Read Joshua 1:1-9.

1. What is the promise God gives Joshua in verse 5?

2. God gives Joshua three commands in verse 7. What are they?

In your own words, what do they mean?

3. What did Joshua experience when faced with the great challenge of leading Israel (v. 9)?

4. What is the Lord's answer to those fears?

Why would that have made any difference to Joshua?

Read Numbers 13:26—14:12 which gives the report of the exploration trip into Canaan taken by the twelve leaders of Israel's twelve tribes.

5. From this passage, what were Joshua's reasons for being willing to go into the promised land?

6. Only two of the twelve leaders trusted God. How did God respond to Israel's lack of courage (14:11-12)?

Why did he respond in this way?

Read Genesis 12:1-4.

7. God works through people to accomplish his purposes. What courage was required of Abraham in response to God's call?

Read Luke 1:26-38.

8. Mary faced severe disgrace by choosing God's way. What was her response to God's messenger (v. 38)?

Read Matthew 26:36-46.

9. Jesus had the courage to do the Father's will. Describe his agony in verse 38.

Describe his resolve in verse 46.

10. *Leadership question:* How has God demonstrated to you, through his Word and work in your life, that he is trustworthy?

How have you failed to believe him?

11. *Response:* The world waits desperately to know God's love. Nations live in darkness, people are dying of hunger, and others are barely surviving in appalling poverty. Millions suffer indescribable pain under the oppressive hand of evil men and women. They do not have hope in Christ. God is calling for courage—courage to live by love, to walk in the light, and to preserve the bond of unity with other Christians. In the context of his tenderness and grace, what do you resolve to do?

Suggestions for Leaders

Leading a Bible discussion can be an enjoyable and rewarding experience. But it can also be intimidating—especially if you've never done it before. If this is how you feel, you're in good company. When God asked Moses to lead the Israelites out of Egypt, he replied, "O Lord, please send someone else to do it!" (Ex 4:13). But God's response to all of his servants—including you—is essentially the same: "My grace is sufficient for you" (2 Cor 12:9).

There is another reason you should feel encouraged. Leading a Bible discussion is not difficult if you follow certain guidelines. You don't need to be an expert on the Bible or a trained teacher. The suggestions listed below should enable you to effectively and enjoyably fulfill your role as leader.

Preparing for the Study
1. Ask God to help you understand and apply the passage in your

own life. Unless this happens, you will not be prepared to lead others. Pray too for the various members of the group. Ask God to open your hearts to the message of his Word and motivate you to action.

2. Read the introduction to the entire guide to get an overview of the subject at hand and the issues which will be explored. If you want to do more reading on the topic, check out the resource section at the end of the guide for appropriate books and magazines.

3. As you begin each study, read and reread the assigned Bible passages to familiarize yourself with them. Read the passages suggested for further study as well. This will give you a broader picture of how these issues are discussed throughout Scripture.

4. This study guide is based on the New International Version of the Bible. It will help you and the group if you use this translation as the basis for your study and discussion.

5. Carefully work through each question in the study. Spend time in meditation and reflection as you consider how to respond.

6. Write your thoughts and responses in the space provided in the study guide. This will help you to express your understanding of the passage clearly.

7. It might help you to have a Bible dictionary handy. Use it to look up any unfamiliar words, names or places. (For additional help on how to study a passage, see chapter five of *Leading Bible Discussions,* IVP.)

8. Take the response portion of each study seriously. Consider what this means for your life—what changes you might need to make in your lifestyle and/or actions you need to take in the world. Remember that the group will follow your lead in responding to the studies.

Leading the Study
1. Begin the study on time. Open with prayer, asking God to help the group to understand and apply the passage.

2. Be sure that everyone in your group has a study guide. Encourage the group to prepare beforehand for each discussion by reading the introduction to the guide and by working through the questions in the study.

3. At the beginning of your first time together, explain that these studies are meant to be discussions, not lectures. Encourage the members of the group to participate. However, do not put pressure on those who may be hesitant to speak during the first few sessions.

4. Have a group member read the introductory paragraph at the beginning of the discussion. This will orient the group to the topic of the study.

5. Have a group member read aloud the passage to be studied. (When there is more than one passage, the Scripture is divided up throughout the study so that you won't have to keep several passages in mind at the same time.)

6. As you ask the questions, keep in mind that they are designed to be used just as they are written. You may simply read them aloud. Or you may prefer to express them in your own words. There may be times when it is appropriate to deviate from the study guide. For example, a question may already have been answered. If so, move on to the next question. Or someone may raise an important question not covered in the guide. Take time to discuss it, but try to keep the group from going off on tangents.

7. Avoid answering your own questions. If necessary, repeat or rephrase them until they are clearly understood. An eager group quickly becomes passive and silent if they think the leader will do most of the talking.

8. Don't be afraid of silence. People may need time to think about the question before formulating their answers.

9. Don't be content with just one answer. Ask, "What do the rest of you think?" or "Anything else?" until several people have given answers to the question.

10. Acknowledge all contributions. Try to be affirming whenever possible. Never reject an answer. If it is clearly off-base, ask, "Which verse led you to that conclusion?" or again, "What do the rest of you think?"

11. Don't expect every answer to be addressed to you, even though this will probably happen at first. As group members become more at ease, they will begin to truly interact with each other. This is one sign of healthy discussion.

12. Don't be afraid of controversy. It can be very stimulating. If you don't resolve an issue completely, don't be frustrated. Move on and keep it in mind for later. A subsequent study may solve the problem.

13. Periodically summarize what the group has said about the passage. This helps to draw together the various ideas mentioned and gives continuity to the study. But don't preach.

14. Don't skip over the response question. Be willing to get things started by describing how you have been convicted by the study and what action you'd like to take. Consider doing a service project as a group in response to what you're learning from the studies. Alternately, hold one another accountable to get involved in some kind of active service.

15. Conclude your time together with conversational prayer. Ask for God's help in following through on the commitments you've made.

16. End on time.

Many more suggestions and helps are found in *Small Group Leaders' Handbook* and *Good Things Come in Small Groups* (both from IVP). Reading through one of these books would be worth your time.

Resources

Campolo, Anthony, Jr. *The Power Delusion: A Serious Call to Consider Jesus' Approach to Power.* Wheaton, Ill.: Victor Books, 1984.

Costas, Orlando E. *Liberating News: A Theology of Contextual Evangelization.* Grand Rapids: Eerdmans, 1989.

Ellul, Jacques. *The Presence of the Kingdom.* 2nd ed. Colorado Springs: Helmers & Howard, 1989.

Kozol, Jonathan. *The Night Is Dark and I Am Far from Home: A Political Indictment of the U.S. Public Schools.* New York: Continuum, 1984.

Kraybill, Donald B. *The Upside-Down Kingdom.* Scottsdale, Penn.: Herald Press, 1978.

Newbigin, Lesslie. *Foolishness to the Greeks: The Gospel and Western Culture.* Grand Rapids: Eerdmans, 1986.

Sider, Ronald J. *Rich Christians in an Age of Hunger: A Biblical*

Study. 3rd ed. Dallas: Word, 1990.

Snyder, Howard A. *The Problem of Wineskins: Church Structure in a Technological Age.* Downers Grove, Ill.: InterVarsity Press, 1975.

Wallis, Jim. *Agenda for Biblical People.* Rev. ed. San Francisco: Harper & Row, 1984.

World Christian. P.O. Box 40010, Pasadena, Calif. 91104.